# Brilliant Activities for Gifted and Talented Children

## That Other Children Will Love Too

Ashley McCabe Mowat

Brilliant Publications

# About the author

Ashley M. Mowat, Gifted Educator and Consultant (M Ed Gifted Education)

Ashley Mowat grew up in the southern states of America and was a student in the gifted programme from the age of 8. She received a BA in Early Childhood Education, a BA in Elementary Education and studied Psychology at Converse Women's College in South Carolina. Following university, Ashley continued her education at Converse, receiving a masters degree in Gifted Education. During this time, Ashley taught in an inner city school and completed a thesis on Underachieving Gifted Males. She also planned and implemented a curriculum for the top 100 gifted students in her area for the Athena Institute, a summer programme for gifted students.

Ashley moved to England, married, and in 1999 taught Key Stage 1 at Gateway School in Great Missenden, Buckinghamshire. The following year, she piloted a gifted programme in the school. She spent the year writing and implementing a themed curriculum dealing with issues of the gifted and talented. The programme has been a great success. Ashley has organized Creative and Critical Thinking Workshops at Gateway during the school holidays and taught at various summer programmes for gifted pupils. Ashley teaches at Gateway part-time. She has provided INSET training days for teachers in schools involved with the Excellence in Cities programme and works with the National Association for Gifted Children (NAGC) on their website.

Ashley is available to provide INSET training days, and workshops for children. She can be contacted direct via email (amm_gifteded@hotmail.com) or via Brilliant Publications.

**Brilliant Publications**
1 Church View, Sparrow Hall Farm,
Edlesborough, Dunstable, Bedfordshire, LU6 2ES

Tel:     **01525 229720**
Fax:    **01525 229725**
e-mail: **sales@brilliantpublications.co.uk**
Website: **www.brilliantpublications.co.uk**

Written by Ashley McCabe Mowat
Cover design by Lynda Murray
Illustrated by Kirsty Wilson

© Ashley McCabe Mowat 2003
ISBN  1 903853 47 8

First published in the UK in 2003.
10  9  8  7  6  5  4  3  2  1

Printed in the UK by Alden Group Limited.

# Contents

# Introduction

Teaching Gifted Children is becoming an increasingly important topic in the UK. A very confusing issue for most teachers is just where to begin! You already have so much to do, and probably can't work out when you are going to have time to include activities for Gifted and Talented Children! However, it is extremely important to reach these children, as they are quite often children who fall behind, lose their confidence and become underachievers.

This book will help you to make a start. It is designed to give you ideas for activities that you can use in your classroom. The activities can be modified to suit ages from 6 and up. The work that the children produce will be extremely different because the activities allow room for creativity and open-ended answers. I have based the activities on Bloom's Taxonomy and the Cognitive/ Affective Domains of Creative Thinking.

Bloom's Taxonomy of Educational Objectives has been widely adopted as a model for conceptualizing higher level thinking skills for gifted learners. Although originally developed for a quite different purpose (to classify instructional objectives and test items in a hierarchical fashion), practitioners began to relate the levels of the Taxonomy to the teaching of thinking skills for gifted and talented youth or for children in general. The model now presents a hierarchy of thinking operations whose highest levels are analysis, synthesis and evaluation and can provide the basis for exciting the child's intellectual processes. You will find a chart explaining these levels on page 6. The activities in this book will stretch the children to think at the three highest levels.

E. Paul Torrance developed the faces and forms of creativity through the Cognitive and Affective Domains. In the Cognitive category are Fluent Thinking, Flexible Thinking, Original Thinking and Elaborative Thinking. In the Affective category are Curiosity, Imagination, Risk-taking and Complexity. I have developed the activities in this book to reach all of these types of thinking skills, and have outlined this for you on page 9.

Gifted Children are not the only children who will benefit from this book. There are activities that cover many types of creative and critical thinking skills that will enable all children to develop their cognitive processes. I think you will find that the best part about this book is that your children will thoroughly enjoy the activities. You could stretch some of the activities out for days or, in the Brainteaser section, just have a quick warm-up to spark interest and excite the brain! You will also have the confidence of knowing that you are doing something extra in your classroom that really helps all of your children THINK!

# Bloom's Taxonomy

Bloom's Taxonomy describes six levels of thinking, arranged sequentially from least to most complex.

1. **Knowledge** is simply recall. Students can say that they 'know' something if they can recall it, recite it, or write it down.

2. **Comprehension** means that students can say what they 'know' in their own words. Retelling a story, stating the main idea, or translating from another language are several ways in which students can demonstrate that they 'comprehend' or understand what they have learned.

3. **Application** means that students can apply what they have learned from one context to another. For example, they may be required to decide when to apply mathematical concepts to real-life situations.

4. **Analysis** means that a student can understand the attributes of something so that its component parts may be studied separately and in relation to one another. Asking students to compare and contrast, categorize, and/or recognize inferences, opinions, or motives would give them experience in analysis.

5. **Synthesis** requires students to create a novel or original thought, idea, or product. All of the activities we call 'creative thinking' give students experience with synthesis. Also, when students can take bits and pieces of several theories or combine ideas from different sources to create an original perspective or idea, they are thinking at a synthesis level.

6. **Evaluation** gives students opportunities to judge what they have analyzed.

# Bloom's Taxonomy

| Knowledge | Comprehension | Application | Analysis | Synthesis | Evaluation |
|---|---|---|---|---|---|
| Remembering previously learned material | Ability to grasp the meaning of material | Applying concepts and principles to new situations | Breaking material down into component parts | Pulling parts together in a new whole | Ability to judge the value of material |
| Lowest level of learning | Interpreting the material | Applying laws and theories to practical situations | Understanding the organizational structures | Formulating new patterns and structures | Use of definite criteria for judgements |
| Listing learned information | Seeing relationships among things | Solving mathematical problems | Analysis of relationships between parts | Abstract relationships | Value judgements based on clearly defined criteria |
| Bringing to mind appropriate material | Projecting effects of ideas | Constructing charts and graphs | Recognition of organizational principles involved | Communicating an idea in a unique way | Highest learning outcome |
| Recalling information | Communicating an idea in a new or different way | Demonstrating correct usage of method or procedure | Requires understanding of both the content and structural form | Creating new or original things | Use of cognitive and affective things together |
| Bringing to mind stored knowledge | Lowest level of understanding | Applying rules, methods, concepts, principles, laws, theories | Analyzing the elements | Taking things and patterning them in a new way | Solution-finding and decision-making |
| Reciting learned information | Explaining ideas | Requires higher level of understanding than comprehension | Problem-finding | Implementation and planning | |
| Remembering terms, methods, facts, concepts, specific items of information | Summarizing material | Making use of the unknown | | | |
| | Understanding facts and principles | | | | |
| | Estimating future trends | | | | |
| | Predicting consequences | | | | |
| | Interpreting charts and graphs | | | | |

**Brilliant Activities for Gifted and Talented Children**

# Cognitive domain/divergent thinking

## 1. Fluent thinking (to think of the most)

Generation of quantity

Flow of thought

Number of relevant
   responses

**Examples of fluent thinking:**
- The person who has a flow of answers when a question is asked
- The person who usually has several ideas about something while others struggle
- The person who always produces more than others in the class
- The person who uses a large number of words when expressing him/herself

## 2. Flexible thinking (to take different approaches)

Variety of kinds of ideas

Ability to shift categories

Detours in direction of thought

**Examples of flexible thinking:**
- The person who thinks of various ways to use an object other than its common use
- The person who shifts and takes another point of view or considers situations differently from others in the class
- The person who has different interpretations of a picture, story, or problem other than one being discussed
- The person who, when given a problem, usually thinks of different possibilities for solving it

## 3. Original thinking (to think in novel or unique ways)

Unusual responses

Clever ideas

Production away from the
   obvious

**Examples of original thinking:**
- The person who is dissatisfied with the stereotyped answer and seeks a fresh approach
- The nonconformist who cannot help being different and always has a new twist in thinking and behaving
- The person who enjoys the unusual and will rebel against doing things the way everyone else does them
- The person who deviates from others to do things his/her own way
- The person who not only questions the old way but will try to work out a new way

## 4. Elaborative thinking (to add on to…)

Embellishing an idea

Stretching or expanding upon
   things or ideas

**Examples of elaborative thinking:**
- The person who always attempts to add details to things and make them more beautiful
- The person who will add lines, colour and detail to his/her drawings or another's
- The person who produces more detailed steps to an answer or solution

## Affective domain/ creative feeling behaviours

## 1. *Curiosity* (to be willing to…)

Be inquisitive and wonder

Be open to puzzling situations

Toy with an idea

**Examples of curiosity:**
- ◆ The person who constantly searches for 'why'
- ◆ The person who questions everything and everyone
- ◆ The person who needs no real push to explore something unfamiliar
- ◆ The person who constantly searches for new ideas

## 2. *Imagination* (to have the power to…)

Visualize and build mental images

Dream about things that have never happened

Reach beyond sensual or real boundaries

**Examples of imagination:**
- ◆ The person who can go somewhere in his/her dreams without leaving the room
- ◆ The person who likes to build images of things she/he has never seen
- ◆ The person who can tell a story about a place she/he has never visited
- ◆ The person who can make inanimate objects come to life

## 3. *Risk-taking* (to have the courage to…)

Take a guess

Defend own ideas

Expose oneself to failure or criticism

**Examples of risk-taking:**
- ◆ The person who will defend his/her own ideas regardless of what others think
- ◆ The person who will admit to a mistake
- ◆ The person who is willing to try the difficult task
- ◆ The person who prefers to take a chance or dare

## 4. *Complexity* (to be challenged to…)

Seek many alternatives

See gaps between how things are and how they could be

Delve into intricate problems or ideas

**Examples of complexity:**
- ◆ The person who appreciates complex problems and ideas
- ◆ The person who wants to work out things for him/herself
- ◆ The person who will choose a more difficult way out

# How the activities relate to the domains

| Activity | Fluency | Flexibility | Originality | Elaboration | Curiosity | Imagination | Risk-taking | Complexity |
|---|---|---|---|---|---|---|---|---|
| Brainstorming | ● | | | | ● | | ● | |
| I wonder | | | | ● | ● | ● | | |
| Do or die! | | ● | ● | | | ● | | ● |
| The magic words | | | | ● | | ● | | ● |
| Who could it be? | | ● | | | | ● | | ● |
| A die-r mistake! | | ● | | | | ● | | ● |
| Twins … or … | | ● | | | | ● | | ● |
| Trickster | | ● | ● | | | ● | | ● |
| A flying nuisance | | ● | | | | ● | | |
| Who is he? | | ● | | | ● | | | ● |
| Quilting memories | | ● | | | | | | ● |
| A dog's life | | ● | | | | | | ● |
| Wacky neighbours | | ● | | | ● | | | ● |
| A carnival wish | | | ● | | | ● | | |
| The big top! | ● | ● | | | | | ● | |
| Sweet Shoppe | | | ● | ● | | ● | ● | |
| The secret clubhouse | | | ● | | | ● | ● | |
| Dinotrocious | | ● | | | ● | ● | ● | |
| Up, up and away! | | | | | ● | ● | ● | |
| Reach out and touch someone | ● | | | | | ● | | |
| Can you see the sea? | ● | | ● | | | ● | | |
| N is for narwhal | ● | | | ● | ● | | | |
| Breakout | | | ● | | | ● | ● | |
| Treat your taste to chocolate | | | ● | ● | | ● | | |
| Futurama | | | | | ● | ● | | ● |
| Cut-ups | | | ● | ● | | ● | | |
| Timmm…ber! | ● | ● | | | | ● | | |
| Again and again! | ● | | | | | ● | | ● |
| Traffic blues | ● | | | ● | | ● | | |
| Newspaper bonanza | ● | ● | | | ● | | | |
| Treasure hunt | | | | | ● | ● | | |
| Rain, rain, go away | ● | | | ● | ● | ● | | |
| Special edition | ● | | ● | ● | | ● | | |
| Sandwich-city | | | ● | | | ● | ● | |
| Where in the world? | ● | ● | | ● | | ● | | |
| The moon or bust! | ● | ● | | | | ● | ● | |
| Inside out! | ● | ● | ● | ● | | ● | | |
| The dilemma | | ● | | | | ● | ● | |
| Peek-a-boo | | | | | ● | ● | ● | |
| Survivor | ● | | | ● | | ● | | |
| It's a lemon | ● | | ● | ● | | ● | | |

## Guidelines for brainstorming

# 1. Quantity is important

Get as many ideas as you can down on paper or on the board. It is not important what you say at this stage, just make sure you have a long list!

# 2. No judgement

Don't make fun of anyone's ideas, even your own. Welcome all ideas and write them down on your list. You will have a chance to judge your ideas at a later stage.

# 3. Favour far out ideas

Ideas that seem really silly are great! They stimulate creativity and may lead to an idea that does not seem so silly later. Good ideas sometimes stem from crazy ideas!

# 4. Bouncing ideas off each other is definitely allowed

When you hear someone else's ideas, it makes a light go off in your brain that gives you a different idea. This is called bouncing ideas off one another. Only one idea can lead to another, and another, and ANOTHER! Sometimes the best ideas are stimulated from hearing a great idea from your friend.

# Ideas for brainstorming

**Name as many items as you can that are:**
- ◆ As important as the written word
- ◆ As impossible to open as a tin without a tin opener
- ◆ As complex as the human brain
- ◆ As intricate as a spider web
- ◆ As often found together as a lock and key
- ◆ As obese as a whale
- ◆ As unusual as a mother with ten sets of twins
- ◆ As insignificant as a grain of sand
- ◆ As frequently used as a Christmas tree
- ◆ As much a pair as shoes and socks
- ◆ As bright as a spotlight
- ◆ As funny as a clown car with ten clowns
- ◆ As happy as a winner at the end of a race

**How many ways can you think of to:**
- ◆ Protect yourself in water
- ◆ Protect yourself from a storm
- ◆ Protect yourself from sunburn
- ◆ Show someone that you like them
- ◆ Please your teacher
- ◆ Please your parents
- ◆ Please a friend
- ◆ Please a sibling
- ◆ Please yourself
- ◆ Keep yourself from getting bored waiting for lunch at school

**How many ways can you think of to improve (to make it better, to make it more fun, etc):**
- ◆ A bookmark
- ◆ A desktop
- ◆ An alarm clock
- ◆ A pocket
- ◆ A refrigerator
- ◆ A coolbox

**Examples of using brainstorming in subject areas:**

**List as many as you can:**
- ◆ Geographic terms
- ◆ Explorers (kinds of)
- ◆ Community helpers

**How many ways can you think of to improve:**
- ◆ Neighbourhoods
- ◆ Mealtimes at your house
- ◆ Recreation facilities in your village or community
- ◆ Understanding between different minority groups at your school/in your community

**How many different:**
- ◆ Kinds of hardships might _____ have faced
- ◆ Ways to use any natural resource
- ◆ Problems might have occurred when …

Use this list for a place to begin and then come up with your own.
Better yet – ask the children to develop their own lists! To target flexibility, have the children categorize their responses.

# I wonder

This is an activity that I do in my classroom that the children always love! You may want to create a box in your classroom for these questions, or simply ask children to write their questions down on a piece of paper. The children can use this activity to find out about any subject that they are interested in!

Have the children write down any question about something that they want to know the answer to. The question should begin with Who, What, When, Where, How or Why. The child will then take the question home and find out the answer. Have the children brainstorm sources. They may use any source available. (For example: encyclopedias, the internet, a parent, a specialist.) The children may occasionally swap questions with classmates.

At the beginning of each lesson, the children will share their findings with the class. This is a time when discussion may be led and the internet could be used to find further information.

**Brilliant Activities for Gifted and Talented Children**

## Do or die!

Two men walk into a restaurant. They both order exactly the same drink. One man drinks it fast and one man drinks it slowly. The one who drinks it fast lives. The one who drinks it slowly dies. WHY?

You can ask as many questions as you would like, but the teacher can only answer yes or no.

## The magic words

Tell the children you are going to draw a perfect picture with a pencil in the air, which you hold in your hand. You are going to pass the pencil around the table and see if any of the pupils can draw a perfect picture as well. You will say yes, or no, and they will pass the pencil to the next person. There is no perfect way to wave the pencil in the air; the trick is to say THANK YOU to the person handing you the pencil. If the pupil receiving the pencil says this, and draws in the air, they have drawn the 'perfect picture'. If they do not say thank you, they have not. You may have to pass the pencil around several times for the children to notice what you are doing.

**Brilliant Activities for Gifted and Talented Children**
This page may be photocopied by the purchasing institution only.

© Ashley McCabe Mowat

**13**

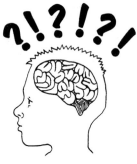

## Who could it be?

Two Australians got on a bus. One of the Australians was the father of the other Australian's son. How was this possible?

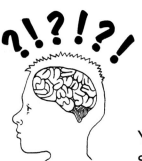

## A die-r mistake!

You are walking through a graveyard when you notice something wrong with one of the gravestones. It says something that isn't true! How do you know that something is wrong with this gravestone?

Here lies Oliver Judkins
11 October 1948 – 15 September 1999

And his beloved widow, Virginia
7 December 1950 – 10 September 1983

**Brilliant Activities for Gifted and Talented Children**
This page may be photocopied by the purchasing institution only.

# Twins ... or ...

Robert and William Parry were both born just before noon on 7 May 2001. They had the same parents, Andrew and Diana Parry. You see Robert and William in the nursery and say to Diana, 'Your twins are lovely!' Diana looks at you and replies, 'They are not twins!' You are very confused. They were born on exactly the same day, with the same parents!

How is this possible?

# Trickster

Your class is taking a trip to the national science convention on Thursday and you can't wait! You wake up in the morning, put your thinking cap on and get ready for the journey. On the bus, you can't stop thinking of all the interesting and exciting new things you will see. There is one exhibition that everyone has been talking about. A science teacher has developed a new secret substance and you really want to know what it is. When you arrive, you make a beeline straight for the exhibit where the teacher is standing. You hear him say, 'Here it is, right in front of you in this glass jar! A new substance that will dissolve any solid matter in just seconds.' Oh my, you think. He is lying! All of these people are being fooled!

How do you know the science teacher is not telling the truth?

**Brilliant Activities for Gifted and Talented Children**
This page may be photocopied by the purchasing institution only.

© Ashley McCabe Mowat

**15**

## A flying nuisance

Mrs Stringer was aiming her can of bug spray at some mosquitoes. They were really beginning to annoy her guests at the annual family barbeque! Half of the mosquitoes flew away, but one returned. Mrs Stringer took careful aim again. Once more, half of the mosquitoes flew away, and one returned. Mrs Stringer was beginning to get very cross, for when she counted them, she noticed that there was exactly the same number of mosquitoes there now as at the beginning!

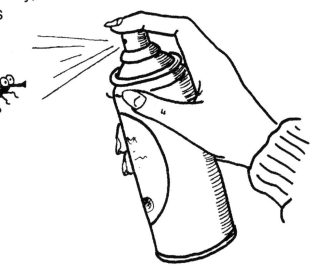

How many were there in the beginning?

## Who is he?

A man was sitting at home watching the news. All of a sudden, he stood up, switched on the light, and began to sob uncontrollably.

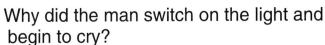

Why did the man switch on the light and begin to cry?

You can ask as many questions as you would like, but the teacher can only answer yes or no.

**Brilliant Activities for Gifted and Talented Children**
This page may be photocopied by the purchasing institution only.

## Quilting memories

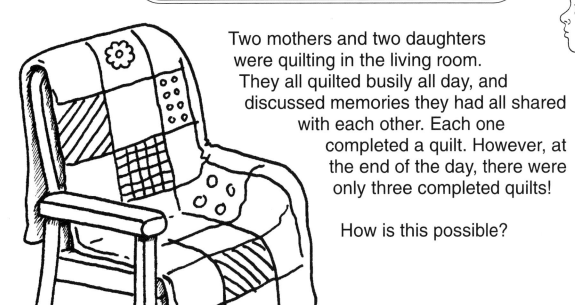

Two mothers and two daughters were quilting in the living room. They all quilted busily all day, and discussed memories they had all shared with each other. Each one completed a quilt. However, at the end of the day, there were only three completed quilts!

How is this possible?

## A dog's life

**For Year 5 and up**

Mrs Gardner decides to take her dog for a walk around 3:00 in the afternoon. She must go before dark, because the dog is very peculiar. He stops at every puddle and Mrs Gardner has to fill a jug with water for the dog to drink. He drinks exactly four litres of water without stopping! More than four litres makes the dog lie down and take a ten minute nap in the middle of the field. With less than four litres, he digs a deep hole in the field that Mrs Gardner has to fill back up again before she can move along! She sometimes wonders why she ever bothered to get a dog to keep her company! Mrs Gardner's main problem is that she only has two jugs, and neither of them holds exactly 4 litres! One of her jugs holds 5 litres and the other holds 3 litres! How does she manage to make sure that the silly dog gets exactly 4 litres every time?

# Wacky neighbours

**For Year 5 and up**

On Zoo Street stand five houses in a row, each a different colour. A man of different nationality owns each house. Each man has a different hobby, a different kind of pet, and each enjoys a distinctly different drink.

I know that the Englishman lives in the blue house, the German owns a pet hippopotamus, tea is the favourite drink in the yellow house, the Italian prefers strong coffee. The yellow house is just to the right of the green house, the man who fixes cars owns a monkey, the tennis player lives in the white house, the man in the middle house drinks water. The American lives in the first house, the one who plays the tuba lives next to the man with an alligator. The man who loves to sing karaoke drinks milk, the tennis player lives next door to the man with the potbelly pig. The Swedish man's hobby is gardening, the American lives next to the red house.

Can you work out who drinks the apple juice and who owns the elephant?

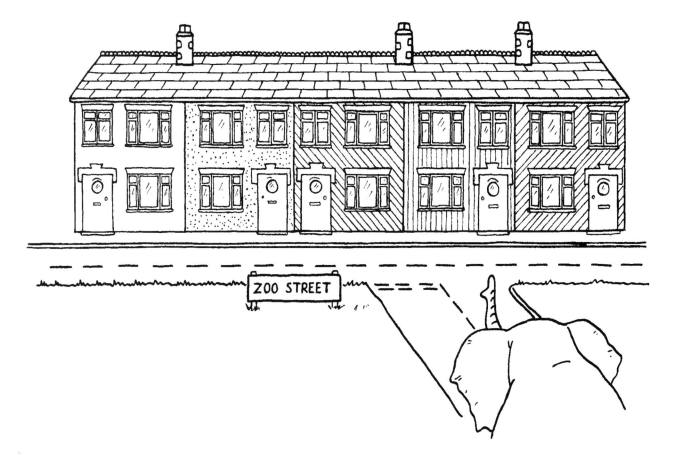

**Brilliant Activities for Gifted and Talented Children**
This page may be photocopied by the purchasing institution only.

# A carnival wish

An amazing event occurred last week when you went to the carnival with your parents! You saw a stand offering a prize for the perfect day. For you to enter the prize draw, you needed a £1 ticket. You reached into your pocket only to find 80p. You were so upset because your parents had given you your limit of spending money and you knew better than to ask for more. However, your little brother was feeling very kind and held up a shiny 20p coin. You took the money and entered the draw, promising to include him if you won.

An hour later, you hear your name over the loud speaker saying to report to the stand for THE PERFECT DAY prize. Your parents look surprised but follow along. You can't believe it! The man in charge says to you, 'We will do everything we can do to give you the perfect day. If you plan it, we will make your dreams come true.'

- ◆ Think of all the things you love to do that would make the perfect day.

- ◆ Where would you go?

- ◆ Why would you choose this place?

- ◆ What would you eat?

- ◆ Would you meet anyone special?

- ◆ What would you do to make this day unique or one that you would remember for a lifetime?

- ◆ Plan the day including meals, activities and entertainment beginning at 8:00 in the morning and ending at 8:00 in the evening. Make sure you have enough time for everything you want to do! And of course, don't forget your little brother!

**Brilliant Activities for Gifted and Talented Children**
This page may be photocopied by the purchasing institution only.

© Ashley McCabe Mowat

**19**

# The big top!

Your best friend has invited you to the circus for his/her birthday! You ask your mum if you can go. She really likes your best friend so, of course, she says, 'Yes, as long as you don't act like a **clown**!'

When you and your friend arrive, you see a table for a prize draw. The prize is for you and a friend to be part of the circus for a day. You enter your name, and take your seat.

You see a trapeze artist, a tightrope, a tiger trainer, a girl who rides on an elephant, and a clown!

Soon, it is the interval and the lights go down! A trapeze artist comes over to the microphone to announce the winner of the draw. The spotlight is on and the drums begin to roll. To your astonishment, she says, 'And the winner is…' and you hear your name!

You can't believe your luck! You take your best friend and go down to the centre ring. Now all you have to do is make a decision.

---

- ◆ Brainstorm all the jobs in a circus.

- ◆ Decide who you would like to be for a day.

- ◆ What would you do?

- ◆ Who would your best friend be? Why would you choose that person? How are you like them? How are you different?

- ◆ How would you want to dress?

- ◆ Which circus job might make you feel uncomfortable? What could you do to make you feel more comfortable in that job?

- ◆ Write a story about what happens to you and your best friend. What is the experience like?

---

**Brilliant Activities for Gifted and Talented Children**

# Sweet Shoppe

You have just won the lottery and want to do something exciting. You are very creative and want to do something useful as well.

You decide that the area where you live really needs a new sweet shop, so you decide to open one. Your shop will be a special place where you create all of the sweets. They will be unique.

You need to create at least five new sweets.

---

◆ Choose a theme for your sweet shop. The children can brainstorm ideas as a class before beginning the activity. Example: space

◆ What will the shop be called?

◆ Describe the new sweets you have created.

◆ What do they look like and how do they taste?

◆ Design the wrappers.

◆ Make a sample menu and tell how much each of them would cost the consumer.

◆ Plan and draw a design of the outside and inside of your shop.

◆ List some of the risks you would be taking to open your own shop. How would taking these risks make you feel?

◆ How will you market/sell your sweets? Decide on a target group and tell how you would implement your marketing programme. (Years 5+)

---

**Brilliant Activities for Gifted and Talented Children**
This page may be photocopied by the purchasing institution only.

© Ashley McCabe Mowat

**21**

# The secret clubhouse

Everyone is always trying to tell you what to do!

You and four of your best friends decide that you want a place that is secret – a place where you can do what you want and you make up your own RULES!

You decide to form a secret club.

◆ What is the secret club called?

◆ What are the rules of the club? How will you make them? How might making these rules make you or any other member feel uncomfortable?

◆ Where would your secret club be? Could you build a clubhouse?

◆ What activities will you do in the clubhouse?

◆ Design the secret clubhouse. Draw the outside and a plan for the inside.

◆ Design a symbol for your club that includes something about each member.

**Brilliant Activities for Gifted and Talented Children**

# Dinotrocious

One afternoon, you are sitting in front of the fire reading your favourite book. Your mum asks you to take the dog, Tommy, for a walk.

You really don't want to put your book down, but your mum has been really busy lately with your baby sister. You grab the lead and Tommy begins to get excited! He knows you are taking him on a walk through the woods! You are on the path when Tommy begins to pull uncontrollably! He has never been so persistent! He begins to sniff around the bottom of a tree covered in large leaves. You try to pull him away but he will not move.

Your curiosity gets to you so you decide to have a look. There before your very eyes is the most enormous egg you have ever seen! You take it home and research the possibilities. After visiting the library and looking through many books, you discover it is a dinosaur egg. It must be the only one in the world! You decide to keep it until it hatches.

◆ Write a story about what happens when the egg hatches.

◆ Why do you decide to keep the egg?

◆ What is it like to have a dinosaur as a pet?

◆ What are some of the problems of having such a large pet?

◆ How do you feed it?

◆ How does it make you feel to have such a unique pet?

◆ What are some characteristics a person needs to be a good pet owner?

◆ How does the new pet affect your family, Tommy the dog, and your neighbours?

**Brilliant Activities for Gifted and Talented Children**
This page may be photocopied by the purchasing institution only.

© Ashley McCabe Mowat

**23**

# Up, up and away!

You are lying in bed one morning and can't seem to sleep very well. Something is sticking in your back and making you feel very uncomfortable. You reach your hand behind your shoulder and feel something that feels like feathers. You sit up and discover you have wings! You are baffled by your new addition! Where did they come from?

You glance over to your bedside table and see a piece of paper that looks as if it is glowing. You pick up the shining piece of paper and read:

*Please look after my wings today. I am on holiday.*

*A fairy*

You know you only have day to use the wings, so you get out of bed quickly and begin to try them out.

---

◆ Write a story about what happens to you during the day.

◆ Where will you go and what will you see? Why would you choose to go there?

◆ If you could take someone with you, who would it be and why would you choose them?

◆ How does it feel to fly?

**Brilliant Activities for Gifted and Talented Children**
This page may be photocopied by the purchasing institution only.

# Reach out and touch someone

A new greeting card company has sent a challenge to all of the children in your school!

---

**Greeting Cards R US**

Dear Children,

*Enter our challenge and you could WIN*
*a tour of our factory!*

We know that children always have brilliant ideas so we'd like to ask you to help us come up with some new greeting card designs!

We are setting up a new subsidiary company, to sell cards produced by children. We'd like you to come up with a name of this new subsidiary and design at least three new cards that are ready for the shelf!

The winner of the competition will get an all expenses paid trip to our super-duper new factory!

So, kids, get your thinking caps on and send in your designs! I look forward to hearing from you.

*Pat Rumplebottom*

Pat Rumplebottom
Managing Director

---

◆ Discuss all types of feelings and reasons for sending a card to someone. How would it make the person sending or receiving the card feel?

◆ Brainstorm all of the occasions to send a greeting card. Which is your favourite? Why?

◆ Choose some occasions from the list or make up some new ones.

◆ Will your cards be happy, sad, funny, a joke, or something else?

◆ Make sure to include all of the elements of a greeting card (the name of your new company with a logo, a bar code, etc). You can brainstorm all of the elements of a greeting card.

◆ Ensure your cards are very creative so that you win the competition!

**Brilliant Activities for Gifted and Talented Children**
This page may be photocopied by the purchasing institution only.

© Ashley McCabe Mowat

**25**

## Can you see the sea?

It is so amazing that the same word can mean so many different things! Some words are pronounced the same, but have different meanings. These words are called homophones. How many can you think of?

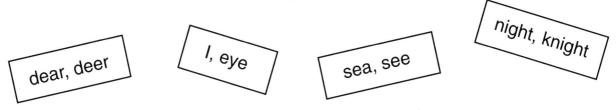

dear, deer

I, eye

sea, see

night, knight

Your favourite children's television programme is having a contest! The contestant must enter a poem that is at least 10 lines long with as many pictures as possible. The poem can be about any topic.

The winner will get to come on the show and read their poem on TV! You really want to win so you must get very creative!

- ◆ Brainstorm a list of words that you can draw a picture for.

- ◆ The words can be homophones or just pictures of the object.

- ◆ Choose a topic for your poem.

- ◆ Get to work!

**Brilliant Activities for Gifted and Talented Children**

## N is for narwhal

Get into a group with some of your friends.

You have seen lists of animals for children to help them learn the alphabet. You see the same lists over and over again. You think that the people that write them are not using their creativity and you think you could do a much better job.

To make things more challenging, you are going to compete with other students in the class to see who can come up with the most creative names for animals from all letters of the alphabet!

- ◆ Find out what a narwhal is!

- ◆ List an animal for every letter in the alphabet.

- ◆ You can name more than one for each letter.

- ◆ You will earn 1 point for each animal which is not used by any of the other groups.

- ◆ The group with the most points wins.

**Brilliant Activities for Gifted and Talented Children**
This page may be photocopied by the purchasing institution only.

© Ashley McCabe Mowat

**27**

# Breakout

You recently moved into a very old house and think today is the day for exploring. You know that an old man and his wife lived in the house for 22 years before you moved in.

There is a set of steps that leads up to the loft and you think that is just the place to begin! When you open the small door to get inside you see spider webs and dust everywhere! There are even very old paintings lying around. In the corner you notice a very large painting of a little girl. You think it is lovely and decide to take it downstairs to show your mum. When you move the painting, you notice a large metal box hidden behind it. You look closely and discover that it is a safe. To your disappointment, it also has a combination lock.

However, today is your lucky day! You see a piece of paper peeping out from under the safe. You open it and see a set of numbers. 3, 6, 8, 2, 5. You try the lock in that order but it doesn't work! You realize that you are going to have to break the code.

- ◆ How many different number combinations can you make with the numbers on the piece of paper?

- ◆ If the combination didn't work, brainstorm a list of alternatives for getting into the safe. Cross out all the ways that might harm someone.

- ◆ What do you find in the safe?

- ◆ Write a story about what you find. Does it link up to the old man and his wife, to the little girl in the painting, or someone else?

## Treat your taste to chocolate

Your local village is having a fete on the green during the weekend. There is going to be a special competition. You have seen posters advertising this all over the village.

You read the rules and go home straight away to tell your mum. Chocolate is your favourite food so you are determined to win that contest!

Work as a group.

Hint: look at some recipe books to help give you ideas.

**HEY KIDS!**

Enter the children's cooking contest on the green...

and win a year's supply of
## CHOCOLATE!

**The rules are as follows:**
1. Create a treat that includes chocolate.
2. The treat must be original.
3. Your recipe must be included with your entry.
4. Each recipe needs to have a creative name.

---

◆ In your group, put together a cookbook with your entries. Include an illustration of each treat.

◆ Come up with an idea for a TV advertising campaign that includes the dialogue, a picture and a slogan.

◆ Remember what caught your eye on the posters for the contest!

---

# Futurama

You can see many films about the future at the cinema. We don't know exactly what the future will be like; however, we can make predictions based on what we know. This is called application.

As you are an expert on what the future will be like, a famous Hollywood director has asked you to come up with an idea for a film that takes place in the year 2100. You will need characters, a setting, a plot, a climax and an ending.

Based on what you know about the future, write a movie script.

◆ What problems do you think people in the future will face?

◆ How will people live?

◆ How will things have changed?

◆ Will the world have become better or worse? How?

◆ Include your main character's feelings about the world in the year 2100.

**Brilliant Activities for Gifted and Talented Children**

# Cut-ups

Cooperating with others can produce very creative results!

1.   Get into a small group with some of your friends.

2.   Your teacher will provide each group with four pieces of sugar paper (one large and three small), masking tape, scissors, a ruler and a pencil.

3.   You have 30 minutes to make all of the objects listed below:

---

◆   An object that holds water

◆   An object that measures a member of the group's height

◆   A name card for the group that is waterproof

◆   A fashionable piece of jewellery

◆   A party decoration

---

Your teacher will award points for cooperation, creativity and completion of the task.

Have fun!

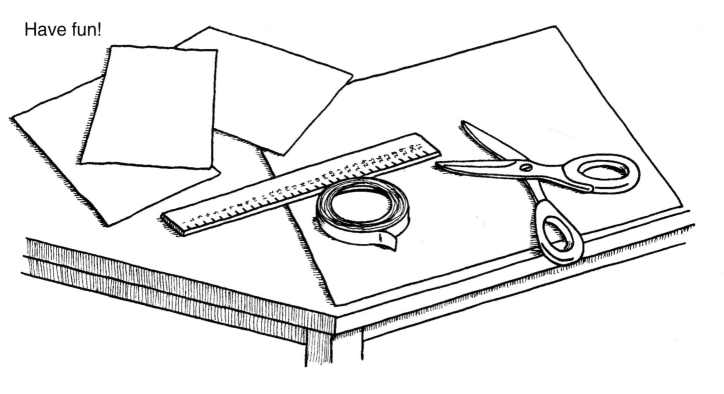

**Brilliant Activities for Gifted and Talented Children**
This page may be photocopied by the purchasing institution only.

© Ashley McCabe Mowat
**31**

## Timmm...ber!

You are very concerned about the rainforests. You have heard that if something isn't done about all of the trees being cut down, there soon will be no more rainforests. You do not want this to happen so you get to work.

- ◆ Brainstorm all of the reasons for saving the rainforests.

- ◆ Make a list of all of the animals that live in the rainforest.

- ◆ Make a list of products that come from the rainforest.

- ◆ Write a letter to the Queen or Prime Minister explaining your position.

- ◆ Design a flyer that will convince people to aid in your campaign to save the rainforests.

- ◆ Brainstorm places that may be ideal to place your posters.

## Again and again!

You are growing more and more concerned about the amount of waste that is being thrown into landfills. You have heard of recycling and you always help, but you think that more junk can be reused. It is just a matter of creativity!

Broken pieces of pottery can be used to make a mosaic tabletop.

◆ Brainstorm a list of things that can be recycled.

◆ Brainstorm a list of items that are not being recycled.

◆ Choose three items off your list and create ways to recycle them.

◆ What interesting ideas can you come up with?

◆ Invent a new use for something that comes from recycled material.

**Brilliant Activities for Gifted and Talented Children**
This page may be photocopied by the purchasing institution only.

© Ashley McCabe Mowat
**33**

# Traffic blues

Beep Beep! Screech. Your mum is taking you to a very exciting birthday party and you are late again! You are going to miss the bouncy castle, bumper cars and the all-u-can-eat ice cream station!

It is so annoying how traffic seems to always get in the way. There must be a better way!

◆ Create a new vehicle that will get you from one place to another without the inconvenience of traffic.

◆ Brainstorm a list of all of the things that need to be on the vehicle. Make sure to include all parts that are necessary for comfort and navigation.

◆ Give your new vehicle a creative name.

◆ Create an advertisement to sell the vehicle.

◆ What are the advantages of the vehicle?

◆ What are the disadvantages?

## Newspaper bonanza

You can get so much information from a newspaper!

Get into a small group with some friends. Your teacher will give each group one newspaper (broadsheet).

Your challenge is to find as many items on the list as possible and glue them onto a large sheet of sugar paper. The items must be labelled in order to receive credit.

You have just 30 minutes, so get started! The group with the most items wins!

### Difficult
- ◆ A number larger than 100
- ◆ A man wearing glasses
- ◆ A woman wearing glasses
- ◆ A picture with a family in it
- ◆ A picture of something that you can travel in
- ◆ The name of an English county
- ◆ The name of a foreign country
- ◆ A picture of something to eat
- ◆ A picture of an animal
- ◆ A picture of a building

### More difficult
- ◆ An advertisement for something electrical
- ◆ A weather report
- ◆ A picture of an important figure in our country's government
- ◆ A picture of an important figure from another country's government
- ◆ The name of a newspaper

### Most difficult
- ◆ A classified advertisement
- ◆ A picture of a member of the royal family
- ◆ An example of maths being used

Try coming up with a list of more things for your classmates to find!

**Brilliant Activities for Gifted and Talented Children**
This page may be photocopied by the purchasing institution only.

© Ashley McCabe Mowat

**35**

# Treasure hunt

Your challenge is to create a treasure hunt in the school grounds.

Decide who the treasure hunt will be for. It could be for another class, or your class could be split into two groups. Find out how many people are in the group.

Your group must go out and choose places to hide the clues and a place for the treasure. You will need one place for each person in the group looking for the treasure.

Each person in your group must write at least one clue that is clever and creative. The clues should give enough information to lead the hunter to the treasure, without supplying the answer.

Make your clues creative by using analogies or pictures. You might want to write your clue as a poem!

Good luck!

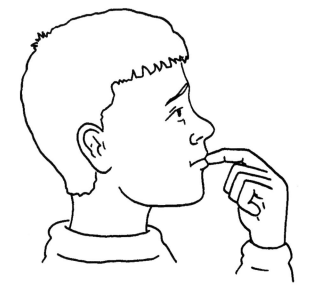

Look for a tree near a place to park…
May be a home to a lark …

Look up and find a hole…
for a clue, not a mole!

**Brilliant Activities for Gifted and Talented Children**
This page may be photocopied by the purchasing institution only.

# Rain, rain, go away

You have three friends over to play and your parents are moving house. This means that all of your games and toys have been packed away! This is OK because you were planning to play outside. To your dismay, it begins to rain when your friends arrive!

The only things you have are a pencil and paper, cardboard, tape and your imagination!

You decide to create a game that you can play indoors with your friends. You decide that the best way to begin is to come up with a theme, like Harry Potter.

- ◆ Create a game that you can play indoors with only the materials on hand.

- ◆ Brainstorm things usually found with a game (game board, spinners, and dice).

- ◆ How will the game begin?

- ◆ How does the game end? (How does a player win?)

- ◆ What is the objective of the game?

- ◆ What are the rules?

- ◆ Create obstacles for your game.

This is the last time you will see your friends for a while, so you want to make your last day together as exciting as possible. Get started!

**Brilliant Activities for Gifted and Talented Children**
This page may be photocopied by the purchasing institution only.

© Ashley McCabe Mowat

**37**

## Special edition

Before doing this activity, your teacher will have asked you to watch the news for homework and make a list of all of the topics that were discussed. Now you will find out why!

Brainstorm a list of all the topics you saw on the news (weather, news, sport, property prices, currency, stock market).

Your challenge is to work as a group to read the news to each other. The catch is that the year is 3023!

◆ Your group is free to come up with as many ideas for news stories as you wish. Each person in the group can write and read more than one.

◆ What are some of the new inventions that have been developed?

◆ Where do we live? Do we live in houses?

◆ What do we use for money? Do we still use pounds?

◆ Invent a new sport that is played in the future using your knowledge of what the future will be like.

◆ Think about what products will be available in 3023. Create an advertisement that will advertise them.

# Sandwich-city

Your good friend, Bill, has just bought a new sandwich shop called Sandwich-city. All of the staff have quit, saying that they just don't want to work for your friend because he is too demanding! Bill decides a machine is much better than staff because he won't have to pay the machine!

The only problem is that he needs you! You are the expert in engineering and creativity. Bill knows that you are the only one who can design a perfect sandwich-making machine.

However, Bill doesn't like paying people so he offers you a free sandwich every time you visit the shop for the rest of your life! You realize this could be very valuable, because you can walk there from your house.

Designing the machine will be fun, as well, because you enjoy a challenge!

- ◆ Brainstorm types of bread and ingredients that could be used in a sandwich.

- ◆ Design a perfect sandwich-making machine.

- ◆ Where do you put the ingredients?

- ◆ How does the bread bake?

- ◆ What are some advantages of having a machine make the sandwiches?

- ◆ What are some disadvantages?

- ◆ If Bill hired someone to work in the shop, what other jobs could they do besides make the sandwiches?

- ◆ Bill also knows that, to encourage customers to frequent the shop, he must have a sandwich that no other shops have! Again, you are the friend with the imagination, so he asks you to create a new sandwich too! After long hours of deliberation, he agrees to pay you for this one, but only if it is a sandwich that is totally new, and tastes terrific!

**Brilliant Activities for Gifted and Talented Children**
This page may be photocopied by the purchasing institution only.

© Ashley McCabe Mowat

**39**

# Where in the world?

Houses are all the same! They are all on roads, all have the same type of rooms and are virtually all built with the same materials. You think they are all rather boring and that someone should invent a new place to live. You praise the people who have heard the beat of a different drummer and built a house that is different!

Your family has decided to sell their house because they want to move. They have been looking at new houses that look exactly the same as your old one!

You have offered to design a new house for them and promise that it will be very different. Now it is your job to design something that your entire family will love.

◆ Brainstorm things that are needed in a place where people live.

◆ Design a new place for your family to live, which is nothing like a standard house.

◆ Where will the dwelling be located?

◆ Will the dwelling have a view?

◆ Use as many shapes as possible in your design.

**Brilliant Activities for Gifted and Talented Children**

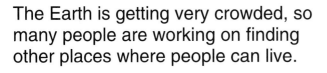

# The moon or bust!

The Earth is getting very crowded, so many people are working on finding other places where people can live.

The moon seems like a great option because it is not too far away to get to from Earth. We know, however, that there is little gravity and no oxygen there. There are also no supermarkets, houses or schools.

If we did go to live on the moon, a living-centre would have to be designed.

◆ Brainstorm all the things that people need in order to survive.

◆ List them in order of priority.

◆ Design a living-centre for 50 people to live and work on the moon.

◆ Plan everything needed on paper and then make a large drawing of the centre.

◆ Make a list of qualifications someone would need to take the risk of leaving home and going to live on the moon. Do they need to be brave? Caring?

◆ Describe the ideal person to become leader of the new moon colony.

**Brilliant Activities for Gifted and Talented Children**
This page may be photocopied by the purchasing institution only.

© Ashley McCabe Mowat

**41**

# Inside out!

Your school is building a new indoor gym. The headteacher really wants to know what the pupils would enjoy in the gym, so she has a competition for all pupils to enter.

You only have a week to complete the design, so you get to work visiting many local gyms to see what they have.

◆ Brainstorm as many things as you can think of that would be needed in a school gym.

◆ Design an indoor gym for your school.

◆ The school wants the most exciting gym possible with at least ten activities.

◆ There is an extra bonus for anyone who invents an idea for a new activity that is unique to your school.

◆ Have a theme for your gym.

◆ How would you design the gym so that it can accommodate a lot of people?

◆ Draw a plan with explanations of what you would like the new gym to contain.

## The dilemma

Your parents have gone out for the evening and have put you in charge of your baby sister, Aimee.

Your parents have told you not to answer the door, and only answer the telephone if it rings once, hangs up and rings again. You are also to feed the dog, Rufus, at 6:00. They leave you with their mobile number, give you and your sister a cuddle, and drive away.

You know that your next-door neighbour, Abby, is having your best friend, Anna, around to stay the night. You also know that your neighbours, Carl and Daneen, are having a loud party across the road. You give Aimee a bath, eat pizza for dinner and settle down with a good book.

All of a sudden, someone knocks on the door, the phone begins ringing and Aimee begins to cry.

Finish the story with three separate endings.

**Suggestions for endings**
◆ You answered the door and learned a lesson.

◆ You didn't answer the door and learned what lesson?

◆ You talk to the person through the door. How did this turn out?

# Peek-a-boo

You have moved into a new neighbourhood and hear that the house at the end of the road is haunted. You are not scared of anything and you really want to explore as soon as possible.

One afternoon, after school, you have some time to explore, so you push open the front gate. You walk closer to the front door and notice that it is open. You slowly push the door open and step inside. All of the furniture is covered with sheets and there are cobwebs everywhere. You walk to the stairs and begin to climb. The stairs are creaking with each step you take and you are beginning to feel a chill. All of a sudden your foot goes through a stair. You step back and look inside. You see a glowing box. This must have been hidden here for ages!

You slowly open the box to reveal a folded white sheet. You wonder what that is doing in the box! You lift up the sheet to see if there is anything exciting under it and notice that you can't see your hand anymore!! You realize that the sheet has made your hand invisible! Just think of the possibilities! You stuff the sheet into your bag and run home.

---

◆ Write a story about what happens when you use the sheet over your body to become invisible.

◆ Will you share it with any of your friends? Why or why not?

◆ What are some of the advantages of being invisible?

◆ What are some of the disadvantages?

◆ What are some ways you could help people?

**Brilliant Activities for Gifted and Talented Children**

## Survivor

The National Consumer Group (NCG) has done a survey that has shown that there are some shops in the UK that claim to sell everything that a person needs to survive. The NCG has asked that all shops agree to a challenge to prove whether this claim is true. It is very good marketing for the shop that is chosen so they all agree to participate.

The challenge is that a person will go inside a shop and live there for a week. The person will not be allowed to leave or take in any possessions. That person is you.

◆ Choose a shop in the UK that you think you could live in for one week.

◆ List all the things you need to survive.

◆ Can you find a shop where everything you need to live comfortably is provided?

◆ Write down a schedule of a day from 7 o'clock in the morning to 9 o'clock at night.

◆ What problems did you face?

◆ Why did you choose that shop?

◆ What are the advantages of choosing that shop as opposed to another one?

## It's a lemon

The Lemon Products Advertising Company is on the edge of ruin. They have not had a sellable product in years. Their motto is, 'If you make it, we can sell it.' However, with products like coats for computers, and toys for houseplants, it is almost impossible. But . . . this is their job and they need to save the company. In an effort to do this, they have asked you to come and help.

The company has even resorted to coming up with its own products to sell because no one wants to use them. None of the adults working for the company has had any good ideas lately so they have decided to try asking children.

Lemon Products needs goods and adverts if it is to survive. Can you help?

- ◆ It is your job to come up with a seemingly unsellable product, and make it appear like a must-have to the consumer. Good luck!

- ◆ Create a TV advertisement that would make people want to go out and buy your product immediately!

- ◆ Create a jingle.

# Answers

## Answers to Brainteasers

**Do or die! (page 13)**
The poison was in the ice!

**Who could it be? (page 14)**
One was the mother.

**A die-r mistake! (page 14)**
Virginia can't be his widow if she died first!

**Twins ... or ... (page 15)**
They are triplets!

**Trickster (page 15)**
The solution would have dissolved the glass jar!

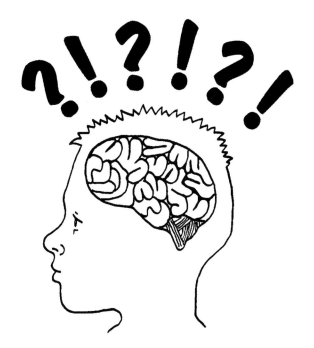

**A flying nuisance (page 16)**
There were two.

**Who is he? (page 16)**
The man is a lighthouse keeper, and he saw on the news that a ship is headed for his point but can see no light. It is inevitable that the ship will crash, which is the man's fault.

**Quilting memories (page 17)**
They are a grandmother, mother and a daughter.

**A dog's life (page 17)**
Fill the jug with 5 litres. From it, fill the jug that holds 3 litres. This leaves 2 litres in the jug that holds 5 litres. Pour out the 3 litres. Pour the 2 litres from the 5 litres into the 3 litres. Fill the jug with 5 litres again. From it, pour into the 3 litres until it is full. 4 litres will be left in the jug that holds 5 litres!

**Wacky neighbours (page 18)**

| American | Italian | English | German | Swedish |
|----------|---------|---------|--------|---------|
| White | Red | Blue | Green | Yellow |
| Juice | Coffee | Water | Milk | Tea |
| Tennis | Tuba | Fixing cars | Karaoke | Gardening |
| Alligator | Pig | Monkey | Hippo | Elephant |

## Answer to Main activities

**N is for narwhal (page 27)**
A narwhal is an Arctic whale that has a spotted pelt and is characterized in the male by a long spirally twisted ivory tusk projecting from the left side of its head. It is also known as a sea unicorn, unicorn fish and a unicorn whale. Sometimes two horns are developed side by side.

**Brilliant Activities for Gifted and Talented Children**

© Ashley McCabe Mowat

# Further reading

*You Know your Child is Gifted When... A Beginner's Guide to Life on the Bright Side* by Judy Galbraith, MA (Free Spirit Publishing)

*Teaching Gifted Kids in the Regular Classroom* by Susan Winebrenner (Free Spirit Publishing)

*Methods and Materials for Teaching the Gifted* edited by Frances A. Karnes and Suzanne M. Bean (Prufrock Press, Inc)

*Teaching the Gifted Child* (fourth edition) by James J. Gallagher and Shelagh A. Gallagher (Allyn and Bacon)

# Bibliography

Adaptation from Bloom's Taxonomy from *Taxonomy of Educational Objectives, Book 1* by Benjamin S. Bloom (Longman Inc, 1956, copyright renewed 1984 by Benjamin S. Bloom and David R. Krathwohl)

Torrance, P (1975). Athens: University of Georgia, USA. For further information see the last two books in 'Further reading'.

# Acknowledgements

I would like to thank a few people for making this book possible for me!
First of all, I would like to thank Joan and John Wade at the Gateway School in Great Missenden, for giving me the opportunity to begin a programme for gifted children at their school. I thank the pupils at Gateway as well for trying out the activities and letting me know exactly which ones they enjoyed the most, providing me with the best possible selection for this book. I also thank Dr Nancy Breard at Converse College and Mrs Bert O. McCabe (my mother and long time teacher of gifted education) for their continuous support, ideas and editing of this book. Lastly, I would like to thank Jo Counsell at the National Association for Gifted Children for giving me the confidence and push to make a few of my resources available to other teachers.

Ashley McCabe Mowat